Not Ready
To Die

Larry was ready:

Patricia Ann Yarber

A wholly owned subsidary of **TBN**

Not Ready to Die: Larry Has Cancer

Manufactured in the United States of America

10 9 8 7 6 5 4 3 2 1

Library of Congress Cataloging-in-Publication Data is available.

B-ISBN#: 978-1-63769-232-5

E-ISBN#: 978-1-63769-233-2

Dedication

I dedicate this book to my sister, Jennifer Hairess Yarber Coleman, who supported, encouraged, and inspired me to continue writing.

Thank you, my dear sister, for your constant encouragement along the way.

Table of Contents

Life Is Good

Hello, my name is Larry. I just want you all to know that life is short, and you never know when or how you are going to die, so make sure, and very sure, that you enjoy the gifts of life that God has blessed you with. Live it to the fullest; give God some alone time to thank Him for creating you when He did, and do not forget to encourage someone with the Word of God along the way. After all, that is one of the reasons why you were created by the Creator. Never forget that your walk with God is very personal. As sure as you were born, you are going to die living this life. Keep the faith so that you can say, "Old Death, where is your sting?" And remember to die in Christ is gain. You have lived with and through Him. Your life should be all about Jesus.

Larry was a hardworking man. He was an accountant, a very busy one. He had his own business, and he worked eleven years by himself before deciding to hire two employees, Jeff and John. Jeff was six feet tall and had brown curly, bushy hair with big round glasses. He was the type most people would call a nerd, but he wasn't. He was a go-getter. He just knew what he wanted out of life, and he kept his head in his books. Coming out of a single-family home and raised by his mother, he had to stay focused. His mother was seven months pregnant when she gave birth to him prematurely. He was only four pounds and fighting for his life, but God had a plan for him. He never knew his father. His father was due to come home, but he got killed in the service before Jeff was born.

John had both of his parents. He was short and stocky. He was like one of those gamers; the guy that knew how to make the game apps and knew how to play all the game online. He even played with groups of other guys, and they played and made money playing. He worked hard and played hard. They both were young and fresh out of college, well-grounded, and very active in their church youth groups. They taught Bible study and other activities to the eighth-grade youth, a total of fourteen students. John and Jeff were best friends. They had something in common by being the only children and going to the same church. Larry was so happy to have them working for him. They were like the sons that he never had. He met them both at the church picnic when they were little boys and watched them grow up to be very respectful young men. They both were full of joy and highly respected Larry as a father figure. When Father's Day came around, they always had a gift and a card for Larry.

When Larry and Jennifer got married, he knew he couldn't have any kids. He was in a bad accident when he was a teenager. Some drunk driver ran through the stop sign and hit him. He was rushed to the hospital, and he found out later that the guy had passed away because of his injuries. Larry laid there in the hospital for three months, paralyzed from the waist down. They told his mom and him that he would never be able to walk or have kids of his own. God had His hands on Larry. It was a slow and long process, but eventually he started walking again.

So, when they got married, she knew he couldn't have kids of his own. They always talked about adopting kids, but they never did. Besides, John and Jeff came over to the house quite often like it was their second home. They both were okay not having any kids. They were so busy with their own life, working and traveling when they could throughout the country.

Larry had lots of clients that he had built up over the years. He was very good at numbers even in college. That was how he became an accountant because numbers came easily for him. He believed God gifted him with that ability with numbers. He really enjoyed what he did. He thanked and praised God often that he had good help. He would always tell John and Jeff that he prayed for them every night, so they would become the men that God has called them to be because they were so faithful working with him. Larry was so thankful to God for the good help that he had been praying for. For quite some time, he knew that the Lord would come through for him. He knew that there was more to life than just work even though he loved what he was doing. Each year, he accumulated more customers. Reality was starting to set in. He had come to realize, at this point in his life, he couldn't do it all by himself.

Larry decided to take a little time off of work because he had been working long hours due to tax time coming up. John and Jeff had taken their vacation time off at the same time. Larry was very tired from working late nights. The weekend was fast approaching, and he knew he had to come back and work more late nights because it was mid-March "tax time." The calls were coming in from his clients to make their appointments to have their taxes done, not to mention the new clients that he would pick up by word-of-mouth from his clients. Larry didn't have to do any advertising because the clients would do the advertising for him. He worked with a big business firm that had lots of workers. Knowing that, he knew that he, Jeff, and John would be working late nights the following weeks, so he decided to take Monday off. He was looking forward to having a long weekend. He put away the files he was working on and said his goodbyes to Jeff and John, for he knew that the office was in good hands. He also reminded them, in case of an emergency, to feel free to call at any time. He took off in his car headed home.

As he drove down the street, he noticed that spring was fast approaching. The winter seemed so long this year. The weather around the Great Lakes could be brutal at times.

The leaves were starting to bud out on some of the trees, and the daffodils were out already along the side of the road. As he drove home, he was thinking Easter was right around the corner and he wanted to get his yard ready. Every spring, Larry got really excited about getting his yard ready. He knew he was going to win the best yard award for this year in his Homeowners Association. He had put his name in for the drawing, and they were going to pick the winner the first week in June. This year, the winner could win a seven-day cruise. They would fly into Miami and spend one night there at the Hilton, then they would board the ship and tour all the other little islands close by. Larry was very excited because he wanted to take his wife Jennifer on a cruise. He had been saving up money to go on a cruise, and this would be perfect. Jennifer worked with her sister. She would work twelve hours each day, four days a week, and every other weekend at the restaurant they both inherited from their parents. The weekends that she didn't work, she would sleep in or would be busy doing something for the church that they attended. The church was small but family oriented. Her grandparents and parents went to that church and they all taught Sunday school, so everyone knew each other.

Larry loved springtime. To him, it was like a new beginning of planning, planting, and plucking up the old things. Similar to the things we need to do for the Lord. A time of repentance where we could start all over with the things of God. Life changing, refreshing, and renewing our relationship with the Lord. Gardening every spring was peaceful and relaxing, and he would make sure he put the fertilizer down at the right time and fresh mulch. He knew that would make the flower bulbs larger and stronger. He would plant all kinds of flowers: ranunculus, daffodils, daisies, and roses. Those were some of his favorites. He also had an herb garden in the back of the house. Each summer, he and Jennifer would take a break and sit on their screen porch and listen to the birds, watch the butterflies, and watch the hummingbirds fly about as they fought over who was next in line to get the nectar. That was so relaxing for them both after a hard day's work. They had lots of wind chimes because they loved to hear the different sounds of the wind chimes as they sat and drank iced tea on a hot summer evening. Gardening was very relaxing for them both.

The following morning when Larry woke up, before his feet hit the floor, he thanked God for another day watching over him through the night. He could smell the scent of coffee that Jennifer was preparing for him. Larry would eat his bacon and eggs. Monday through Friday, he would just drink his health drinks, so the weekends were very special to him.

Jennifer was off that weekend, and she was up and at it. She had her plans for the day to go to the gym for a couple hours before she went to the church to volunteer in the food pantry that she would do every second Saturday of the month.

She was excited because afterwards she was going to spend the rest of the day with her sister Peggy and her friends that she hadn't seen in a while.

Larry asked Jennifer to make him a big pitcher of lemonade before she left for the day. She said okay and reminded him that she was going to the gym, then stopping over at the church for a few hours, and then spending the rest of her day with her sister Peggy.

Jennifer told him that he needed to put on a long sleeve shirt or lots of sunscreen lotion and his sun hat so he wouldn't get sunburned like he always did every spring and summer. He gave her a big hug and kiss then told her that he loved her more then she could ever know. She smiled at him and told him that she loved him, too, and that Jesus loved him more. Then she took off.

Then he poured his lemonade into a stainless steel cup with ice, put the cap on it tightly, and took it outside with him, placing it on the picnic table before going into the garage. He got out the fertilizer and mulch. He got down on his knees in the flower garden and remembered that he did not put on his kneepads, so he got up went back into the garage to look for them. They were nowhere to be found. He looked under the extra bags of dirt that he picked up from Home Depot when they had a huge thirty percent off sale last week on lawn bags. He couldn't find his kneepads anywhere, so he decided to make some homemade kneepads. It came to his mind that he had watched a YouTube video where this guy had made kneepads out of newspaper and an old rag, so Larry got the newspaper, folded it up, and placed it on his knees. Then he placed the rag on top of the newspaper and tied the string around it tightly. He said to himself, "Thank God for YouTube. These are better than nothing." He put on his working gloves and began to work on his garden. He stopped for a minute to drink some of his lemonade. It was a bit sweet because the ice had not melted down as it normally does with honey, but he thought nothing of it and drank it all.

Shortly after that, he began to work in the garden. He started to feel sick to his stomach, lightheaded, and his vision was getting cloudy. He said, "Lord, help me," and then he decided to stop putting down the flower bulbs. He took off his gloves and sun hat and went inside to wash his hands. He didn't put anything away because he was sure he would be back later to continue. He washed his hands and his face and took off his dirty clothes to lay down across the bed. He didn't bother to pull the cover back.

As he laid there, he looked up to the ceiling, and it was as if the room was spinning. He could hear his heartbeat inside of his head. Then, suddenly, his stomach started to get really upset. He felt the urge to go throw up, so he got up and stumbled his way into the bathroom. As he fell on his knees to throw up, he could feel his blood pressure going up, and he began to pray and ask God to help him and to heal him of whatever was going on in his body. He got up and went back to lay down. He thought to himself he should have just drank his health drink as usual, but it was the weekend and he just wanted to have his eggs and bacon as always. Larry's eyes began to get heavier and tired. He nodded off fast to sleep, but, when he woke up from the nap, he looked over at the clock. It was one o'clock, and he wasn't feeling any better. He felt very hot, so he went into the bathroom and took his temperature. It was one hundred and five degrees. He turned on the cold water to splash it on his face. As he looked at himself in the mirror, he noticed his eyes were bloodshot red and his face was pale. He started to think in his mind, "What in the world is wrong with me? I don't get sick. I feel like someone just hit me over the head with a hammer!" He began to talk to God, asking Him to help. "Father God, I need You to heal me now in the name of Jesus."

As Larry struggled to get back into the bedroom, he held tightly to the door frame so he wouldn't fall. He laid there thinking back-and-forth in his mind if he should call Jennifer. He knew that, by this time, she was at her sister's. He didn't want to bother her because he knew that she had been looking forward to spending quality time with each other. The restaurant was very successful, so successful that they had to hire more workers to work, but he felt bad. He had no choice but to call her on her cell phone, but it just went right to voicemail. He laid there and thought to himself, "What is Peggy's phone number?" As he struggled to remember, he dialed a few numbers, but they weren't the right ones. He finally found the right number to call. Jennifer just happened to answer the phone.

She had looked at the caller ID, so she knew it was him. She picked up the phone and said, "Hi, Larry. What's going on?" He explained to her how he felt, and he told her he had a temperature and his eyes were red. Jennifer said, "Okay! Honey, I'm on my way." What she didn't know was that Larry had passed out before he hung up the phone.

Jennifer was having a good time at the ladies' networking party that her and her sister had been planning for months, where some of their college girlfriends tried to come together once every two or three years. She was disappointed, not at Larry, but she hadn't seen some of her friends since her college days because some were out of the country. One of her best friends was from England. But Jennifer had a sick husband at home that she needed to go see about. She got Peggy's attention, and they went into another room to talk. She told her Larry called and wasn't feeling good, and he had a high temperature. She told Peggy that she wasn't sure that she would make it back. Peggy told her to be careful driving and to be safe, because she knew her sister had a glass of wine. She wasn't a drinker but was just socializing with some of her college friends. Peggy told her that they should pray before she left, so they did. "Father God, please get my sister safely home and give her peace, letting her know that You are with her and her husband in Jesus' name. Amen." Jennifer told her that she would call her to let her know what was going on with Larry as soon as she got a free minute, and then she took off.

On her way home, she began thinking. "What in the world

could be wrong with my husband? He never complains about anything. He's in good health. He is a runner and runs five miles every morning. He is very health-conscious and eats mostly vegetables and fish and very little starchy foods. He is very disciplined when it comes to his eating habits, something that I can never do. But it was the weekend, and he only ate pork on Saturday, so he ate his usual bacon, eggs, and toast. He is a very easy man to please," she thought to herself as she drove down M139 Street. She ran through a red light, and she noticed just up ahead there was road construction going on, so she decided to dash through a neighborhood to bypass the construction. Little did she know, there was an officer clocking her on one of the side streets. She didn't see him at all. He was just sitting there, but he notified his partner that was parked on the main street a few blocks up the road, letting him know that she was on her way towards him in a blue Kia truck. She was coming his way at top speed in a community neighborhood.

As she was headed toward the main street, not paying any attention to how fast she was going, only thinking of Larry being home by himself. She was desperate to get there to see if he was okay. On the other side of the road, there was a police officer parked at the light. She was not paying any attention. She didn't see him, but he saw her. He put his lights on as she passed him. As Jennifer drove through the neighborhood at top speed on to the main road, she happened to look in the rear-view mirror, and she saw the flashing blue lights coming her way. She looked down to see how fast she was going and realized that she was going over the speed limit.

Her heart started to pound. She began to sweat. "Oh, my God," she said to herself as the tears began to fill her eyes. All she could do was think of her husband home alone. She needed to be there for him. As she pulled over, she reached for her purse because she knew that the officer would be asking for her license. To her surprise, it was not there. She had just realized that she had left it at her sister's house. As she slowly came to a complete stop, she looked in the rear-view mirror at the officer getting out of his car. Her mind was beginning to race. "What if the officer doesn't believe me? I'm just trying to get home to see about my husband. I'm sure he hears this story all the time when someone is speeding, and not to mention the fact that I had something to drink!" Then she started to panic as she remembered she had a glass of wine and a couple of watercress sandwiches at her sister's. Jennifer wasn't a drinker, but, at the time, she knew a little wine would do her stomach good.

Paul said, "Drink no longer water, but use a little wine for thy stomach's sake and thine often infirmities" (1 Timothy 5:23 KJV). She had a small shot glass of wine at least twice a week because of the health benefits or when her and Larry go out on special occasions. She began to pray, "Lord, please, I don't want to go to jail for having a glass of wine. My husband is home alone sick, and I need Your help, please." As the officer approached the car, he tapped on the window. She began to slowly roll the window down.

"Lady! Do you know you just passed me doing fifty-miles-an-hour on a thirty-five-mile zone?"

"Sorry, Officer," she said. As she looked at him, the tears began to come down her face. It was as if she didn't have any control over her feelings. At this point, she noticed his name tag: Officer James. So, she took a deep breath, and she tried to explain to him that her husband was home and she had to get home to see what was going on with him. He asked her what her name and her address was, and then he asked for her license and registration.

Officer James said, "Oh! I know your husband. He does my taxes every year. I couldn't drop them off at his office, so he gave me the address and I dropped them off at your house. I remember that address but give me a minute. I have to do my job. I have to go and check anyway. I don't want to get fired from my job, and I have to follow up on this paperwork, so give me your license ma'am. I will do this as quickly as possible."

As she tried to explain, she said, "Officer James! I left my purse at my sister's home because I was in a hurry to see about my husband." She began to explain to the officer what was going on with her husband, and she asked Officer James to call her husband on her cell phone to verify what she was saying. She reached into the glove compartment to get her registration out and gave it to him. Her conscience was bothering her so badly that she had that one glass of wine and was driving. She just knew that the officer could smell the wine on her breath.

19

She thought to herself that he wouldn't notice by looking into her eyes because she had been crying. He said, "I don't think that it is necessary to call your husband. I will be right back, ma'am." He proceeded to walk back to the car to check her registration.

She reached for her cell phone in her jacket to call home, but little did she know, as Larry had gotten up to go back into the bathroom, he had passed out from the pain. She couldn't reach him. The officer returned, and she began to plead with the officer to take her home to see about her husband. The officer asked her to please calm down as he handed her a ticket for driving through a red light and over the speed limit. He told her that he was sorry to hear about what was going on with her husband, and he would be calling for an ambulance in advance, and hopefully it would get to the house before they did.

She looked at him and said, "God bless you, Officer James." He smiled and told her to buckle up and to follow him because he would be driving in front of her with his flashing lights on so they can get to the house faster. He also said she needed to be careful because they were going over the speed limit. She began to put her seatbelt on and prayed for Jesus to take the wheel. She took a deep breath. "Oh, God! Please, look after my husband Larry. He is one of Yours, but we still have a lot of living to do down here, Lord, so please whatever is wrong please make it right in Jesus' name. Amen!" She knew that they were only fifteen minutes away, but it seemed like thirty minutes had past when she got there.

As she began to get out of the car, she asked Officer James if he could help her. She was so nervous, she felt herself trembling. Officer James got out and went to the door with her. As she began to put the keys in the door, she began to feel strange. She knew something was wrong, terribly wrong. As she ran through the living room and down the hallway, there was Larry laying on the floor in front of the bathroom. His eyes had rolled to the back of his head.

She began to scream. "Larry! Larry! Please, wake up! Oh, my God, what is going on?" The officer asked her to step aside and asked her to call 911. He had realized that Jennifer was so upset, she gave him the wrong address. Either that, or he had called it in wrong. He needed to see that Larry had a pulse. Meanwhile, Jennifer ran to the house phone to call for help. She began to explain to the operator what was going on and that she needed an ambulance right away. The operator apologized and told her that the ambulance should be there in less than five minutes or so. There had been a mix up on the address, so she hung up the phone and ran back to see about her husband.

Jennifer told Officer James that the ambulance was on its way. He told her Larry was alive, but he didn't tell her that he could barely feel his pulse. He didn't want her to know how serious it was. At this point, he was hoping and praying also. He was hoping Larry would make it to the hospital alive. The officer could see that Larry hit his head against the wall. There was a big knot on the back of his head filled with blood. He asked Jennifer to get a Ziploc plastic bag and fill it with ice and bring a clean towel, so he can place it on the knot that was on Larry's head. She got up and began to run into the kitchen and looked in the kitchen drawer and grabbed a large Ziploc bag, then she opened the freezer door and filled the bag with ice. She rushed back down the hallway to give the ice bag to the officer, and she stood there and watched as he placed it on the back of Larry's head. She was sitting on the floor, holding his hand and praying. "Lord, please help us. We need Your help."

She could hear the ambulance coming in the distance. She got up and ran to the door. She could hear the sound of the ambulance getting closer on the other side of the neighborhood. She ran out into the street to flag them down, so they knew which house they were coming to. Before the two paramedics could get out of the van, she began to cry. Almost losing her breath, she said, "Please! Save my husband!"

The paramedic looked at her and said, "Ma'am, please try to calm down." He could see that she was hyperventilating and very upset as she tried to gasp for air to breathe. One of the attendants put an oxygen mask on her and stayed with her in the living room, so she could calm down and breathe better. The other paramedic went to see what was going on with Larry. The officer told him what was going on with Larry. The paramedics took his vital signs and put an IV on him. As Jennifer slowly began to catch her breath as normal, the paramedic told her he needed to go and help his partner out with her husband and asked her to just sit there and keep calm, and he would be back to check on her. She shook her head, implying that it was okay to be left alone.

As he began to walk toward the other paramedics, he told him he needed to go get the stretcher out of the van, so he turned around and headed towards the van to get the stretcher. The paramedics slowly placed Larry onto the stretcher to take him to the hospital. The other paramedic went back in the living room to check on Jennifer. By this time, Jennifer had caught her breath and calmed down. The paramedic told her that they were headed to the hospital and asked if she wanted to ride along with them or drive on her own. She told them to please go, and that she would be following them in her car. She thanked the officer for assisting her with everything and locked up the door and left to follow the ambulance to the hospital.

On the way there, she decided to call her sister Peggy on her cell phone to let her know what was going on and to ask her to grab her purse that she put in her closet in the bedroom. Peggy told her that she would grab her purse before she left and would let the ladies know what was going on. She said they will be praying that all will go well, and Peggy told her that she would meet her at the hospital as soon as possible. Peggy knew her sister would be fine because she was a woman of faith, and she knew that God would be there to comfort her and Larry in their time of trouble. They both grew up in the church and went to Sunday school every Sunday. They were very active in church. They both were Sunday school teachers and also had the family restaurant that they ran. Peggy was remembering, when they were younger, how she and Jennifer served in their parents' restaurant on Thursdays when the homeless people came in, and they waited tables that fed the hungry people. That was their parents' way of giving back to the community, and that it was a service of the Lord. Their parents were no longer alive, but both Peggy and Jennifer kept the restaurant up and running.

After Peggy hung up the phone with Jennifer, she told the ladies at the party what was going on with her sister and she needed to go as soon as possible. One of the ladies suggested that they all should hold hands and pray. Peggy began to pray, "Father God, in Matthew 18 [NIV], it says 'Where two or three gather in my name, there I am with them.' Father, we are going to believe that all is going to go well with Jennifer and her husband. That You are already there with them. I ask You to give Jennifer's husband the strength that he needs to go through this. Lord, You said in Isaiah 41:10 [NIV] 'So do not fear, for I am with you; be not dismayed, for I am your God. I will strengthen you and help you; I will uphold you with my righteous right hand.' Lord, please restore his health and give him peace in Jesus' name. Amen." They all got their belongings and took off at the same time.

As Jennifer drove behind the ambulance, she was praying and asking God to have mercy because she had a good husband, and they had a lot more living to do. Her mind began to wander, thinking back on all the years they have been together. She was in her last year in high school, and he was a freshman in college when they first met, before they began their twenty-five years of marriage. It was love at first sight. She knew that Larry would be her husband, and he knew that Jennifer would be his wife. He told her that the first time they met standing at the hotdog station. Her heart leapt. He was six feet tall with medium sized brown eyes and was very smart. They met at a football game hotdog station, where they found out they went to the same church and have been talking ever since. Larry went off to college to get his degree in accounting, and she stayed home to help with the family restaurant and went to a local college. They always kept in touch. Larry came home on holidays, and they would hang out together and catch up with what was going on in each other's lives.

As they arrived at the hospital, the ambulance parked at the door of the hospital, and she parked right behind the ambulance. As the parking attendant ran up to her to get her keys to park the car, she grabbed the ticket he gave her, and she grabbed Larry's hand as they took him right in, telling her he needed to go in for surgery. She quickly kissed him on the lips as she watched them wheel him through the double doors for surgery. She stood there in shock for a minute. She was completely overwhelmed, and she began to gather her thoughts on what to do next. She walked over to the reception desk to fill out the paperwork and give them her husband's medical history. There was not much to give because he had never been in the hospital before. He was in good shape from working out three times a week, was not overweight, and he ate all the right foods.

The receptionist asked her, "Is your husband's name Larry?"

"Yes," Jennifer said.

"Please sit down. Now, this won't take long. I need a little bit of information. I need your husband's insurance card and a little bit of his history."

Jennifer told her there wasn't much history concerning his health because he was in good shape. When she finished the paperwork, she went and sat down and thought to herself, *Sometimes, it seems when you do all the right things something goes wrong, but I know God is in control.*

Then down the hall came Peggy, asking, "Jennifer, what is going on?"

"I don't know. It's been over an hour. The doctor hasn't come out to tell me anything yet! They just took him right in for surgery the minute we got here, so I'm just waiting and praying."

Three hours had passed. Then, down the hall, the doctor came to introduce himself. "Hi, I'm Doctor Frank. Which one of you is Larry's wife?"

Jennifer said, "I am. How is my husband?"

He said, "He is going to be fine. He is in some discomfort, but he's okay. We removed a tumor that was attached to his pancreas. It was about the size of a tennis ball. We think that it is a benign tumor. It seems that we got it all, but there are tests that we are running to make sure that nothing got into his blood system. It doesn't look like a malignant tumor, the aggressive kind, but we want to make sure that it's not. However, he is out of it and not in any pain now. He will be closely watched for the next twenty-four hours. They will put him in a recovery room so he can be watched for about an hour. As soon as they get him all set up, you may go and see him. One of the nurses will come to get you and show you where your husband is."

She thanked him. The doctor excused himself and went on his way to his next patient.

Peggy grabbed her sister and gave her a tight hug and asked her if she wanted her to go in the room with her. Jennifer said, "Yes. Let's go to the hospital chapel, and we can say a prayer for Larry. God can heal him in an instant. We will believe that together."

Peggy began to pray, "Father God, we come to You and ask You to touch Larry's body and to heal him from the top of his head to the soles of his feet. Father God, he said to ask You anything, so we're asking You for a complete healing miracle on Larry's behalf. Father God, I ask You to touch my sister with Your peace that surpasses all understanding, to give her the strength and the courage to go on, knowing that You have everything in control. These blessings, we ask in Jesus' name. Amen." They walked out of the chapel and next to it was the coffee shop, so they went into the coffee shop and grabbed a cup of coffee and chatted a little bit before they decided to go back up to the floor that Larry was assigned to. As soon as they got off the elevator, a nurse came to show them the room that Larry was in. They went in, and he was hooked up to a heart monitor machine and an IV drip that was giving him his pain medication. His face looked a little pale because his blood was low, but they could see that he would be just fine. He wasn't in any pain.

Peggy was one of the prayer warriors at their church. She felt the need to lay hands on him and began to pray for Larry. "Father God, we come to You and ask You to touch Larry's body and heal him from the top of his head to the soles of his feet. Father God, we are asking for a complete healing, to perform a miracle on Larry's behalf. Precious Lord Jesus, You came into the world to heal. We curse any abnormal cell, abnormal growth in Larry's body and command them to die at the roots and leave Larry's body now. In the name of Jesus Christ, Father, I ask You to touch my sister with Your peace that surpasses all understanding and give her strength and the courage to go on, knowing that You have everything in control. These blessings we ask in Jesus' name. Amen." They both said, "Amen!"

The Holy Spirit came in the room. They could fell the Spirit of the Lord. They both felt so much better after they prayed. Larry was sound asleep and didn't know anything that was going on around him. Then Jennifer told her sister that she would be spending the night with her husband at the hospital. They had a nice reclining chair that could lay back like a bed.

Peggy said, "If you need anything, just give me a call. I don't care what time it is. Just call."

Jennifer said, "Okay! I might need you to go by the house to pick up some extra clothes for me, but I will call you to confirm that so you do whatever you need to do. I will call you later." They hugged, and Peggy took off. The nurse came in to check on Larry to make sure he was fine. His blood pressure had gone back up to normal, and his skin color was fine. Although he was in and out of consciousness, the nurse assured Jennifer that he was fine. She said he was heavily medicated, so he wouldn't feel the pain and if she needed to go home or anything it would be okay. He wouldn't be missing her because he probably would be waking up sometime in the night.

Jennifer gave Larry a quick kiss on his lips and grabbed her purse. As she began to walk down the hall, she noticed the receptionist that took her information. They looked at one another, and the receptionist asked if everything was okay with Larry. Jennifer told her he was out like a light and that she was leaving for a quick minute to go pick up some things from home. They stood there for a little while longer, and the receptionist told her that she would definitely be saying a prayer for her before she went to bed. Jennifer said please do, and she continued to get on the elevator.

She looked outside and could see that the sun was about to go down. She stepped outside of the door and enjoyed the fresh air that blew on her face. She took a deep breath and convinced herself that everything was going to be okay. She got into her car and took off and was headed for home. When she got home, she got her and Larry's toothbrushes, his slippers, and his robe and hair brush. Before she left, she decided to turn the nightlights and the alarm on because she knew she wouldn't be returning home that night. She decided to stop in at Wendy's to grab her a salad at the salad bar and some fries and a coke to go and take it back with her to the hospital and eat there because she didn't want to be away from Larry any longer than she needed to be.

It was a long night for Jennifer. She tossed and turned in that chair all night. She got up from time to time to check on Larry. She would just stare at him and watch him breathe. She put her hand on his forehead and rubbed his face. His color had returned. She gave him a kiss, then she prayed and asked God to bless Larry and to give him strength. She got back into the chair and laid down for another thirty minutes, then the nurse came in and introduced herself.

"Hi, Jennifer! My name is Sue. I'm the night nurse. I came to check Larry's temperature and blood pressure, but I would like to know how are you doing. I know it can be very hard on the other person than the one that is admitted. Did you get any rest?"

"No," Jennifer said as she used the remote control to lift the chair back up from the laying position. "The chair was comfortable, but I didn't get much sleep. As they say, there is nothing like your own bed, but I'm hoping and praying that my husband will be okay."

Nurse Sue said, "Don't worry," then she began to take his blood pressure. Larry was totally knocked out. She said, "He's in good hands here, and I know the Lord will see you through. Could you please fill out this breakfast form for me, so he can get a breakfast in the morning?"

Jennifer said "Yes."

"I'm a believer, and I pray for all my patients that I see. I don't tell them all that because they don't believe like I do, or I should say I believe in Jesus Christ and there are so many different kinds of beliefs. I just wait for the opportunity to speak when I hear them speak of Christ."

Jennifer said, "Yes, I totally understand what you are saying. It's a different generation now, and the world seems to be changing every day. There are all kinds of religions, but people don't believe they need a relationship with Jesus Christ, the Son of the true and living God. If Satan can twist the words of God around to deceive Eve in the garden, he can twist your words around here on the earth. 'For we wrestle not against flesh and blood, but against principalities, against powers, against the rulers of the darkness of this world, against a spiritual wickedness in high places' [Ephesians 6:12 NIV]. We as believers have to keep praying and interceding and standing in the gap."

Nurse Sue said, "Amen. Don't get me started talking about the Lord. We will be having some church in this room! I love talking about the Lord." After finishing taking Larry's vitals, she told Jennifer, "It looks like his blood pressure was a bit high. I did check his chart, and it was normal earlier. I don't know why, but we will give him something to lower it."

Jennifer asked, "Is he going to be okay?"

Sue said, "Yes. We are running more tests to make sure everything is good, and the doctor will be in first thing in the morning to check on him." She then asked, "Did he wake up anytime during the night?"

Jennifer told her, "No, I don't think so, but I nodded off from time to time, so I'm not really sure."

Just as the nurse was leaving, Larry started to awaken. She introduced herself to Larry and asked him how he felt. He told her he had a headache and felt nauseated. She explained that it was the medication that was making him feel nauseated, and she would give him something for that. She also explained that his headache was from his blood pressure being up a bit, and she would also give something for that. She needed to go to her medical cart that was in the hallway, so she stepped out of the room and got his medication and came back in quickly.

Jennifer looked into Larry's eyes and told him that she loved him, and everything was going to be all right. He looked at her with his weak eyes and nodded, "Okay."

He fell back asleep. The nurse came in and put the medication into his IV drip. Jennifer asked, "Why is he sleeping so much?"

She said, "It is the pain medication. Do not worry, we heal best when we sleep." The nurse told Jennifer, "If you need anything, just push the call button, and I will be in right away.

Jennifer said, "Okay, I'm going to try to get some sleep." She got back in her chair and fell asleep.

Awake The Next Day

The night had passed, and Larry woke up and began to think to himself. *Lord, what is going on? I remember getting sick in the garden and calling Jennifer and laying down.* Larry laid there, thinking to himself, *I really need to get a closer walk with God. In your mind, it tells you that your close, but your heart really knows you should be even closer as you age. I didn't go to church every single Sunday, but I grew up in a Pentecostal church, and I believed in all the gifts that God have given us, and I do believe in Jesus as my Lord and savior, and I also know that He could heal me if I believe.*

Then he started to pray, 'Father! Forgive me of my short comings, my sins, and iniquities, for I have fallen short and today I want to rededicate my life to You, Lord. I choose to lean on You and ask You to order my steps in the way that I should go. I choose to trust You with my life for the rest of my life, I believe that You are working on my behalf. I won't put my confidence in what I see anymore, but I will totally put my trust in You and read Your Word daily. In Your Word, it says, 'Then they cried out to the LORD in their trouble, and he delivered them from their distress' [Psalm 107:6]. Deliver, my Lord, deliver me. Amen."

Just as he finished praying, Jennifer woke up, and Larry was looking at her with a smile on his face. His eyes were bright, and his skin color was back. She said, "You look like your old self, Larry!" He smiled back!

He asked, "How are you doing, honey?"

She was so surprised. She told him, "At first, I was not so good coming home finding you on the floor in the hallway, but I'm much better now that you're back. I just thank God that you're okay."

"I was laying here when I woke up, trying to figure out what had happened to me. What got me here to the hospital? I only remember bits and pieces."

All of a sudden, he started to feel nauseated again. Jennifer looked at him and asked him what was wrong. He told her that his stomach was getting very upset. Then the nurse came in. Jennifer told the nurse what was happening and that he felt sick. She told them both that it was probably his pain medication, that it was probably a little bit too strong, and she would have to give him a lower dose. She told them she would go get some 7-Up for his upset stomach.

Then, the doctor came into the room and introduced himself. "Hi, Larry. My name is Doctor Frank. Let me look at your charts quickly, and I will explain what is going on. Okay, it looks like your blood pressure is normal. I had to do an emergency surgery on you. You were in a lot of pain when they brought you in, and we removed a tumor that was attached to your pancreas. Some cancer cells can move into the bloodstream or lymph nodes, where they can spread to other tissues within the body. This is called metastasis. Unlike benign tumors, malignant ones grow quickly and can spread to new territory in a process known as metastasizing. We are waiting for the test to come back to make sure, but as you know, you will need to see me as your cancer specialist from now on so we can follow up. I will leave you with a list of doctors that are qualified for this type of cancer, or if you like, you may continue to see me when you're ready to check out. The information to my office will be on your paperwork."

"So, how are you felling today, sir?" asked the doctor.

Larry said, "I'm trying to process everything you just told me, Doctor. Give me a few minutes please. I'm feeling a little weak and nauseated right now, but the nurse went to get some medication for me. She said it's expected for me to be a little exhausted, but I will soon get my strength back."

"Yes, sir," The doctor said. "We're going to keep you another two to four days. It all depends on how fast your wounds heal. Okay. I'm going to check your temperature and blood pressure again, and the nurse will go over some instructions with you that you need to follow once you are released."

The doctor continued to check Larry's vitals. "Well, so far your temperature and blood pressure are good, and if we can keep your blood pressure down, that would be great."

So, Larry would stay overnight.

Larry told Jennifer, "I am thanking God, but I am also shocked that doctor told me I have cancer. I just don't understand. I exercise and eat all the right things. Why is this happening to me?"

Jennifer took his hand and smiled and gave him a kiss. She said, "Larry, you *had* cancer. They removed it, dear. You know God is still good. He could have taken you when you hit your head and fell to the floor, but I believe He has given us more time together to enjoy one another. It has been thirty lovely years, and our love for one another is stronger than ever."

Larry said, "Yes! It's been twenty-five lovely years being your husband. Absolutely wonderful, and I'm honored and very thankful to God. When I woke up this morning, I rededicated my life to the Lord, Jennifer. I asked Him to forgive me for not being a faithful person to Him and that I will do better."

Jennifer looked at Larry, and she could see that he was very serious and knew that he would be a changed man once he got out of the hospital. She knew that his relationship with the Lord would be on a new level. "Give me your hand, so I can pray for us." Larry prayed, "Heavenly Father, You have promised to be our guide. I thank You for giving me a loving wife. Please continue to bless her with strength in all that she does and keep her in the palm of Your hand. Father, continue to give me strength and good health. I pray that Your Holy Spirit will lead and guide me as I continue to walk with You. These blessings, I ask in Jesus' name. Amen."

Larry Is Ready To Go Home

A few days had passed, and Larry was getting better each day. Larry heard a gentle knock on the door. It was the doctor and the nurse coming to see how his wounds were healing. Larry said, "Come in." Larry had just happened to finish watching *The 700 Club*. They had been speaking about healing, and he touched and agreed with the prayer that they prayed concerning healing. Larry prayed that his body was healed, and that the cancer would never come back. The doctor and the nurse said their good mornings, and they asked Larry if it was okay to lay his bed back so they could check his wounds.

He said, "You're the doctor."

They opened Larry's gown and looked at his wounds. The nurse looked up at the doctor and said, "Wow! I've never seen such a wound that healed so fast." She looked at Larry with a smile and said, "The Lord is truly on your side."

Larry had a big smile on his face and lifted his hand, saying, "Hallelujah! Praise the Lord! My God is truly a healer for all sickness and disease. Thank you, Jesus." They both agreed that his wounds were looking good and healing faster than they had ever expected. The doctor also told Larry that his tests came back negative, and his blood pressure looked good, but he would always have to go every six months to get his blood tested for at least a year.

Nurse Sue asked, "Did you have a bowel movement today?"

Larry said, "Not yet. It's still early. Usually after breakfast I have one."

She said, "Okay. Make sure you let me know so I can put that on your chart. It's important that you have one before you leave. That medication you're on can cause constipation really bad. I will give you a stool softener to help."

Doctor Frank said, "Larry, you can be released after breakfast."

She went over the instructions that they needed to follow to take care of his wounds and told him when to take his medications. She told him to ring the front desk and let her know when he had a bowel movement. Larry said okay, and then she left. The breakfast aid Cindy and Jennifer came in at the same time, and she said, "Good morning. Larry, this will be your last breakfast here in the hospital. It was a pleasure serving you. I brought one of your favorites." Cindy walked over to the table tray to place Larry's breakfast. Eggs, toast, and coffee for Larry. She asked Jennifer if she could get her anything, and

Jennifer said, "Yes, please."

"Coffee or tea?"

Jennifer said, "Just coffee, thank you." Larry blessed his food and thanked God that he was getting ready to go home.

Ten minutes later, the nurse came in the room to check on him and told him to stay close to the bathroom. "It will work in about ten or fifteen minutes," she said. "I know you guys are ready to go home."

Thirty minutes past, and she came back. He told her he had just finished coming out of the bathroom, and she said great. She asked them if she could pray for them. He said, "Yes, please."

"I pray to the Father that He may grant you and Jennifer with strength in your inner beings and with power through His Spirit to stay strong, and you both keep the faith." She shook Larry's hand and gave Jennifer a big hug and left.

Jennifer said, "Praise the Lord! That is the best news ever. I woke up in the middle of the night last night. I couldn't sleep at all. I was hoping and praying that all will go well for you today. Larry, I just could not go back to sleep, so I just got up and thanked God, then I went into the kitchen at home to get me a cup of coffee and some toast and started cleaning up. I put fresh sheets on the bed and also the bed in the spare room just in case the mattress on our bed was not comfortable."

Larry said, "Thank you, dear. Hopefully that's not necessary. I haven't been in my own bed for a few nights, but we'll see."

Jennifer said, "I also put the crockpot on before I left. I thought we would have some homemade chicken and dumplings."

Larry said, "That sounds good."

"By the time we get home, it should be ready," Jennifer said. "Just in time for lunch." Jennifer looked at Larry and smiled and gave him a kiss, then they both thanked God for healing Larry so fast.

Jennifer started to pack up some of Larry's things she brought in, like his gardening magazines, house shoes, brush, toothbrush and toothpaste, and his favorite robe that didn't open up from the back. She put them all in his bag. Larry walked slowly out of the bathroom. Jennifer could see that he was a little exhausted. He asked her to help him get dressed. She said okay. He slowly put one arm in his shirt. She came over and helped him with the other sleeve and buttoned his shirt. He sat there on the edge of the bed, he winked his eye at her, then said, "I'm good." She put both of his feet in his pants, and he stood up and fastened them. He closed his eyes tightly because the pain was coming back. It was time to take another pain pill. In spite of the pain, he was ready to go. There was a slight tap at the door. It was the nurse's aid with the wheelchair ready to take him downstairs to the car. Jennifer went ahead to pull up the car at the front door. She parked the car and ran around to the other side to open the door. They smiled at each other. She closed the door and thanked the nurse's aid for all her help and went on their way.

Larry said to Jennifer as she pulled the car into the garage, "I'm so happy to be back home."

She said, "Yes, it's good to have you back home. Although, you must take it easy. You can't do anything for the next eight weeks." Jennifer walked to the passenger's side of the car to help Larry get out. He slowly turned his body around with his feet in front of him, putting one foot on the garage floor, then the other one. They finally made it in the house. She asked him how he was feeling. He said that he was very tired and needed a glass of water. He took a few sips and set the glass down on the table next to him. She told him that she needed to go to the bedroom and get it set up quickly. She would be right back.

She had the room set up with flowers and a bunch of get-well balloons and cards, welcoming him back home from family and friends. She had finished and went back into the living room to get him. Slowly walking into the room, Larry's face lit up with surprise. "Oh, my God, honey. What is this?"

"We all just wanted you to know that we all love and missed you. We can read the cards later."

Larry looked around the room and noticed there was a small bell on the nightstand where he could ring for help when he needed it. She said, "Yep, that is just for you. Now, I will help you undress, and you lay down for a bit."

He asked if it was time to take another pain pill, and she asked if he was in pain already. He said, "No, I just don't want to wait for the pain to come before I take another pill." She reminded him that he could have Tylenol in between the pain-killers. He said, "Okay. Give me one Tylenol, please. I'm exhausted."

Jennifer fluffed up his pillow and kissed him on the forehead. "I'll be right back. I'm going to get the Tylenol." Larry took a deep breath as he pressed his head into the pillow. He started thanking God for allowing him to be back home and in his own bed. Jennifer came back in with the Tylenol and a glass of water. He took one and asked her to place them on the nightstand and told her that he would take another one later when he got up. He had gotten comfortable and didn't want to move out of that spot. He said, "Thank you, my love. You are truly a gift from God." He smiled at her, and then he said, "I need to talk to you about something, but now isn't the time."

She said, "Okay, dear. We'll talk soon."

She went into the kitchen and turned the oven on. She decided to bake a string bean casserole to go along with the chicken and dumplings. Suddenly, tears started streaming down her face. It felt as if she was having a nervous breakdown. She never told Larry how she felt, that if something happened to him... She kept her feelings to herself, and she began to feel an emptiness in her soul, a great loss. Then, she began to see the vision of Larry dying enter her mind for that moment. She said to herself, "Lord, are You trying to tell me something?"

She wiped the tears from her eyes and began to talk to God, thanking Him for giving her the strength and blessing her husband to be back home. Then, the burden lifted off of her shortly after she finished praising God. She put on some praise music and continued preparing dinner. She went to check in on Larry. He had woken up from his nap. She asked him how he was feeling. He said he was tired and very hungry with a smile on his face. She took the table tray out, so he could sit in his recliner chair and watch TV and eat. It was getting late, so Larry made his way back into the bedroom and brushed his teeth. He said his prayer as always. "Lord, I'm so thankful for today. Please watch over me in the night. In Jesus' name. Amen."

Jennifer went to the kitchen to put the leftovers away, and then placed the dishes in the dishwasher. She was thinking to herself that it was nice to be home for the next couple of weeks with Larry. She turned the light out, walked out of the kitchen into the bedroom, looked at Larry sound asleep, and then she went to the bathroom to brush her teeth and take a shower. She said her prayer in the shower and went to bed.

The next morning at the breakfast table, Larry told Jennifer he wanted to talk to her about the life insurance that he had and what she would be receiving when he passed away. "As you know, we don't know the day or hour when we leave this world, crossing over into the next, so we need to get this out of the way."

That made Jennifer so upset, she lifted her hand, saying, "Wait a minute, wait a minute. I don't want to talk about death. I'm just not ready."

But Larry insisted that they talk about it because he told her he needed to make sure that, just in case anything was to happen to him, she would be financially stable and not lacking anything. Then, he grabbed her hand and kissed her. Wiping the tears that were coming down her face, he told her that he loved her so much and he didn't want her to want for anything. And that he strongly believed as a man of God that was his duty to make sure she would be okay. Jennifer said okay, that she understood.

Larry had a kind heart. He was the kind of man that would bring flowers home just because he liked to see her eyes light up and the smile on her face. They would take time out for dinner as if they were still dating after so many years of being married. He said, because she was such a good wife, he didn't want her to wear herself out. He believed she worked just as hard as he did. They would take a picnic basket to the beach and go swimming and sit out there all day, watching the sailboats and feeding the seagulls and pigeons. They went for long walks together on the lakeshore. They did most things together. She would come home sometimes, and he would have the table all set up for a candlelit dinner for two with fresh flowers. He would put on old music that they both loved and enjoyed, and they would dance all around the house, laughing and talking about how they missed each other for that day. They kept their marriage alive when those special times would come up for them to be together. They would never talk about work or anything that would interrupt that moment. They never wanted to lose the fire that they had in their marriage. Even as they grew older, one of them would always come up with creative ways to enjoy the moment. It was something like, when you love the Lord and are excited about the first time giving your life to Him, you want to be pleasing in His sight, not disappointing the Holy Spirit.

Now, when God calls you by your name, and you say, "No, God, I'm busy, not now." When He just wants to spend time with you, you prefer to watch TV, be on Facebook or Instagram, saying, "I'll get with you later." You lose the passion you once had for the Lord, grieving His Holy Spirit. May we never forget those days when we are on fire for the Lord and want to be in His presence, spending time with God puts everything else in perspective. "Does a young woman forget her jewelry, or a bride her wedding dress? Yet for years on end my people have forgotten me" (Jeremiah 2:32 NLT).

Six Months Later

Six months had passed. Larry had gone back to work and life as usual, but one day, he was working in his office and started feeling strange. He couldn't put his finger on it, but he just wasn't feeling like himself. He didn't say anything to Jennifer when he got home because he didn't want her to worry, so he thought nothing of it. The following morning, Jennifer went off to work as she always did, getting up before him. Larry laid there, looking up at the ceiling because he wasn't feeling good. He thought to himself, *What is going on?* He began to see a vision as he looked up to the ceiling. He was seeing a butterfly inside a cocoon, fighting trying to break free and get out. *Why am I feeling like this?* he thought to himself.

He decided to call to make an appointment. They told him to come in right away that same day for a checkup. He called Jeff, and told him that he had a slight pain in his body, and he needed to get it checked out. He might be taking a little time off. He wasn't sure, but he would be getting back with him later on in the day because he had an appointment.

Jeff said, "Okay, boss. Don't worry about the office. We got this. Take all the time you need. As you know, we will keep you posted on what's going on here in the office. We will be praying that all is well and will talk to you later on this evening."

Larry decided to not tell Jennifer what was going on with him because he didn't want her to worry. Larry went into the doctor's office the following day and took all the tests that he needed to take. Jennifer was not aware of what was going on at this point. A few days had passed, and he had been waiting for the doctor to call him back. He was working from home.

Alone one evening after work, while Jennifer was out doing some grocery shopping, the phone rang. It was the doctor calling to tell Larry he needed to come into the office as soon as possible so they could discuss his results and to bring his wife with him. Larry said, "No problem, I will be in tomorrow afternoon at two o'clock if you have an appointment open."

The doctor said, "Yes, that's fine."

It hit him like a bombshell. He thought to himself, *The cancer has returned. They told me they got it all. This cannot be! What is happening?* He felt his blood pressure begin to go up. He started to feel sick to his stomach at the thought that the cancer had returned. He didn't hear Jennifer come in. He still had the phone in his hand when Jennifer entered the kitchen, coming in through the garage door. She never noticed that he had the phone in his hand as she went on about how crowded the store was, and then he hung up the phone.

She asked him, "What is wrong?" Then, she noticed his face was pale as if he saw a ghost. Larry told her he hadn't been feeling good, that he went to the doctor without telling her, and the doctor had just called and said he needed to come back into the office for the results and to bring her along.

Jennifer repeated what he said, "Bring me with you?" Jennifer continued to bring the groceries in from the car. In her mind, she was praying, "God, please! God, have mercy. Please, don't take my husband." Larry began to help her with bringing the groceries in, and she didn't say a word to him. Larry said, "Jennifer, didn't you hear what I just said?"

She replied, "Yes, Larry! I heard what you said, honey! I just need a minute to gather my thoughts and pray."

She told him that she was disappointed that he didn't tell her what was going on. He began to apologize, telling her that he was sorry. He didn't want her to worry about him, and he had been praying and talking to God about it. "I am believing in God for my healing, and I'm not going to say out loud what it could be. I'm going to wait for the doctor to tell me." Then all of a sudden, the tears began to roll down his face, and he told her that he didn't think things were going to get better this time and that he saw a vision of a butterfly fighting to get out of a cocoon. He believed that he was that butterfly fighting for its life, trying to get out, and he also had a dream about being in heaven. Jennifer began to walk towards him as she could see her husband had completely broken down with fear, and he had every right to be afraid.

She was afraid also, but she knew she had to keep it together for him, so she grabbed him and began to pray. "Father God, first we'd like to thank You for this day. This is the day that You have made, and we will be happy in it no matter what is going on in our life. God, You are the giver of life. We just ask You, Lord, to give us peace and strength and to heal my husband's body, for there is nothing too hard for You to do. We thank You, Lord, and will forever give You the praise. In Jesus' name. Amen!"

Larry hugged and kissed Jennifer, thanking her for being so strong for him. He said, "I can say with my mouth that I have faith, but in my mind, the feeling just came over me, and all of a sudden it hit me like a hammer in my gut. I guess it's because the thought of leaving you alone… it's too much for me to bear." He apologized to her for breaking down like he did.

She said, "You're just tired and need to get some rest."

He said, "Yes, you're right. I'm feeling a little weak, but I think I just need something to eat."

Okay!" Jennifer said. "Go and rest on the couch, and I will put some lunch on." She reached for the remote to turn the TV on for him, hoping that would take his mind off of himself for a few minutes until she got lunch ready. "What would you like, Larry?"

He said, "Just give me some chicken soup and some crackers."

As Jennifer began to put the soup on and put the groceries

away, she began to cry. Feeling the warm tears starting to run down her face, she grabbed onto the refrigerator door handle to keep herself up. She fell to the floor crying, and she began to scream into the dish towels she had in her hand. "Jesus, Jesus, Jesus!" That was the only word that would come out of her mouth. "Jesus, Jesus, Jesus!" She knew that God is able, but will He do it again? "Lord! Give me strength and give me peace, so I can be strong for my husband, and please put the right words in my mouth so I can speak encouraging words to my husband. Life and death are in the words that we speak, so I ask You to put Your words in my mouth to keep both of us encouraged. These blessings, I ask in Jesus' name. Amen!"

She managed to pull herself together and called Larry and asked him to come into the dining room, so they could have lunch. He got up off the couch and slowly came in the dining room and sat down. She told him that her work schedule was changing, but seeing that he has a doctor's appointment to-morrow, she wouldn't go in at all. She would call her sister to let her know what was going on.

Jennifer called Peggy and told her she needed to change her schedule completely around, or better yet, just to take her off the schedule and work it out with the rest of the crew. She would get back with her to let her know when she could come back to work. Jennifer also told her that Larry was her first pri-ority at the moment. Peggy said it was no problem, she totally understood, that she would be praying for her and Larry, and that they would be talking soon.

Just as Larry finished eating lunch, he started to feel a little better. He told Jennifer, "Thanks for the chicken soup. There's always something good about chicken soup when you're not feeling well." Jennifer looked at him and smiled and told him that she was happy that he felt better, but it was such a beautiful, sunny day.

She asked, "Why don't we both go and sit on the front porch and get some fresh air?" She could come back in later on and take care of the dishes, so they both went out and sat on the porch, listening to the birds chirp, watching the butterflies fly by.

Larry said, "Jennifer, I will never forget this moment."

"Yes, I'm sure we will not. It's such a lovely day."

Larry said, "I must be honest with you. I'm not looking forward to going to the doctor tomorrow."

Jennifer said, "Me either, but you know as usual, I'm gonna be right by your side, and we will get through this just as we did the first time. God says He will never leave us nor forsake us both. He will be with us until the end. We both have to continue to trust and believe that this is going to work out for good. I don't know how yet, and I don't know when, but we have to continue to trust in Him, the author and finisher of our faith. We both know living down here is not our home, and we have to always be ready, for no man knows the day or the hour when their time is up. We have lived a good life together, so if I should die before you, you will have lots of good memories."

Larry looked at her and smiled and said, "Wait a minute, I'm the one going to the doctor tomorrow."

She said, "Yeah, I know. I'm just saying." Jennifer told Larry that she was going to go in and load the dishwasher up. He told her he was going to sit there for a bit and enjoy the beautiful day. Jennifer immediately got on the phone and called Peggy to let her know what was going on. She needed to pray for Larry and put him on the church prayer list immediately.

Peggy said, "Wait a minute, Jennifer. What is going on? I thought you were past all of this. That the cancer was gone."

Jennifer said, "Yes, I thought so, too, but Larry went behind my back to the doctor's office and did not let me know what was going on with him because he did not want me to worry."

Peggy said, "What kind of nonsense is that? He did not let you know? We could have had his name on the prayer list."

Jennifer said, "Yeah, I know, but he was trying to protect me, and I kind of understand what he is saying. I'm very scared this time that it's going to come and stay. I might lose my husband this time. Things just don't feel right in my spirit. I love him so much. I'm not ready for him to go. I can truly say I have my moments where I break down myself."

Peggy said, "Don't worry, Jennifer. God has everything in control. He said He would never leave you nor forsake you and

Larry. He loves you both, and He won't put any more on you two than you can bear."

Jennifer said, "Yes, Peggy. Thank you so much. I really appreciate your kind words. You always say the right things to me to uplift me when I'm feeling weak and that gives me strength. I love you, my dear sister. Keep us both in your prayers, and I will keep you posted. Tomorrow, I will get back with you." They said goodnight to one another, and Jennifer hung up the phone.

She had finished cleaning up the kitchen and walked back outside on the porch. Larry had nodded off fast asleep. She gently touched him on the shoulders, saying, "Larry, wake up, so we can go inside and you can go to bed." He agreed, so they got ready for bed and did their normal routine: showered, brushed their teeth, prayed, and went to bed.

The Cancer Was Back

Sunday, March 6, 2016

11:23 AM

The next day, Larry got up early and went into his office and prayed for strength for that day. He did his thirty minutes of devotion, keeping his promise with the Lord that he would have a closer relationship with God. He would pray and command his day, saying out loud, "This is the day the Lord has made. I will rejoice and be thankful for it and find strength." However, he did not forget this was the day that would change the rest of his life.

Jennifer laid there for a few minutes. The Spirit of God prompted her to get up and pray. She knew Larry's routine and that he would be out of the bedroom for at least an hour, so she got out of bed and got on her knees and prayed. "Father God, I stretch my hands to Thee. No other can help that I know. Help me walk through my fears by facing them instead of being paralyzed by them. I want to take Your hand and trust Your heart with all that is within me. Give me courage as I stand by my husband through this today and give him peace and strength, letting him know that You will never leave him nor forsake him. This, I pray in Jesus' name. Amen!"

Then, Jennifer got up and went into the bathroom to brush her teeth and shower. When she finished, Larry walked into the bathroom. She could see the fear in his eyes. She didn't say anything to him at the time, but prayed once again to herself that God would see them through this. By the time Larry showered and shaved and came out of the bathroom, she was in the bedroom, dressed and ready. Larry told her she was beautiful as always. She looked at his face, and it was like he was a new man. She could see the peace of God all over him.

She said, "Thank you!" and told him that she was going down to fix breakfast. She went to kiss him, and he grabbed her tightly as if it was going to be the last time he held her. They stayed that way for a couple of seconds and did not say a word. Then, he kissed her and told her he would be down as soon as he got dressed. She looked into his eyes and told him that she loved him and went down to fix breakfast.

She went downstairs and turned on the radio to listen to the news, weather, and traffic report. As Jennifer finished fixing breakfast, Larry sat down to drink his coffee and eat his toast. He told her he hoped that the doctor's office visit wouldn't be too long because he had things to do.

She said, "What is it that you have to do?"

He said, "I need to go to work. There are a lot of clients waiting to get their paperwork back so they can mail their taxes off."

Jennifer asked, "Are Jeff and the other guy helping at the office?"

Larry said, "Yes, but I still need to be there, and it helps me to keep my mind off of myself."

Jennifer said, "Yes, I understand." Jennifer thought to herself, *There's no way he's going to go to work today.* She knew he was just saying that to convince himself that he could go back to work today.

They got in the car and took off and arrived at the doctor's office in no time. Larry walked into the office and opened the door for Jennifer. She sat down, and Larry went up to the window to sign in. The receptionist greeted him and asked him for his insurance card. She took it and told him it would be a thirty-minute wait because two other patients were in front of him. Larry said okay and took a seat. He looked around, and there was a lady sitting there that had lost all her hair because of the chemo treatment. She was talking to the young lady that was sitting next to her.

Larry assumed that was her daughter. They looked just alike, except the younger woman had hair. The mother looked a little fragile, but she had a nice smile. She looked at him, and said, "I'm going to be okay. We have a good doctor, and with the Lord's help, we will get through this!"

Larry smiled back at her, and said, "Yes, ma'am! With the Lord's help, we will." Jennifer looked at the woman and smiled and asked her how long she had cancer. She told her for three months, but she was in remission, and she was just there for a routine checkup.

Before Jennifer could introduce herself to the lady, the nurse came out to get her. It was her time to go in to see the doctor. She smiled at the lady and continued to read a magazine. Jennifer looked at Larry and asked him if he was okay, for she knew what he was thinking about his hair falling out due to the chemo treatments.

Larry's hair was thick and full for a man his age. She knew he wouldn't like it if he lost his hair. Some of his friends from college that he kept in contact with had lost all their hair due to their age. He smiled and said, "Yes, everything is fine." Larry picked up the *Better Homes & Gardens* magazine and began to look at the flowers. He told her that he had just planted some of those that they had in the magazine. She smiled at him, and then the door began to open. The nurse called his name. He looked at Jennifer, and the nurse said that she could come with him. So they walked halfway down the hall into a small, cold room. She was so glad that she remembered to wear her sweater.

The nurse asked him to get on the scale so she could get his weight, and then she wrote it down and asked him to have a seat and roll up his sleeve so she could get his blood pressure and take his temperature. She told him that his blood pressure was a little high, but she told him not to worry too much because most people's blood pressure goes up when they're in the doctor's office anyway. She told Larry that he had lost ten pounds, and asked if he was aware of it. Larry told her, "Yes, but I thought that I had lost the weight because I was exercising all the time." Larry was sitting there, thinking to himself, *Yes, I know it. The cancer was back, and I was praying and believing for God to heal me once again, but I guess that is not His will for me. Yes, I know it is what it says, but to die with Christ is good. I'm not ready to die. I love living, I love my wife and my life, and I'm not ready to die.*

Then, the nurse took him and Jennifer into another room and asked them to have a seat. She said, "Doctor Frank will be in shortly to see you."

Jennifer looked at Larry and said, "I thought you looked a little thin, but I didn't say anything. I thought you were losing weight because you were working out all the time. I'm sure that's probably all it is." She looked at him and smiled.

He said, "Yeah. My appetite has also changed. Food just don't taste the same. My taste buds have changed quite a bit."

As they were sitting there, they heard some papers shuffling around in the hallway. Jennifer whispered to Larry and said, "That's the doctor about to come in." There was a quick knock on the door, and it opened. As soon as she saw the doctor, Jennifer began to feel lightheaded. She knew her blood pressure was going up, and she didn't have a good feeling about this visit to the doctor's office.

"Hi Larry, how are you doing today?"

"I'm doing fine, Doctor Frank. This is my wife, Jennifer,"

"Yes, I remember her from the hospital. Yes, ma'am! How are you today?"

Jennifer said, "I'm fine! Thank you, Doctor Frank, but I'm very concerned about my husband, how is he doing?"

Larry was looking at the doctor when Jennifer asked. He could see the doctor's face, and it didn't look good. The doctor looked at Larry and said, "Larry, I'm sorry to tell you this, but the cancer is back. By the looks of it, you only have about three to four months at the most. But we're going to do everything we possibly can to fight this."

Jennifer grabbed Larry's hand but didn't say a word. She continued to listen to what the doctor was saying. Larry looked at Jennifer, then looked at the doctor, and thought to himself, *My God, I'm not pulling out of this one this time. The cancer is back, and it's going to take me out. Lord, I know we're not supposed to question You, but why? What are You doing? I feel hopeless, and there's nothing we can do about it.*

Larry looked at the doctor and said, "Yes, I hear what you saying, doctor. The sooner I start some kind of treatment plan, the less pain I might be in, but Jennifer and I will discuss what we think is best, and we will get back with you."

"Okay," said the doctor. "But you need to get back with me as soon as possible, Larry. We need to start your treatment plan. Remember, this is an aggressive type of cancer. I'm just a doctor that has looked at your lab work and gave you the diagnosis. God can change this around, and I will certainly be praying that He will step in and turn this around. He has done it before, Larry, for some of our other patients, and He is the same God. Keep your faith in times of trouble, my friend. May the peace of the Lord rest in you and Jennifer always."

Larry said, "Yes, Doctor. Thank you for the kind words. I am dying. This cancer is now spreading throughout my body, and all I can do now is pray. Seeing that this will be my last few months, I need to decide if I want to be treated in the hospital or have hospice come over to care for me." Larry told the doctor and Jennifer that he had made his peace with God, and that, whatever was going to happen, he would be okay with it if that was God's will for him to die with cancer.

Jennifer was sitting there with tears in her eyes, listening to what Larry was saying. In her mind, she wanted to cry out loud and tell Larry to stop saying those things, but in her heart, she knew that he was telling the truth. Maybe that was what she needed to hear to be able to help him, so they both could come to peace with this. In here, he said that he had peace, but that was easy to say. They both had to walk in it, and Jennifer was not there just yet. She knew she had to prepare for what was going to happen.

Larry stood up and shook the doctor's hand and told him that he really appreciated the things that he had done for him, and he would call the office tomorrow to speak with the nurse on the decision that they would make concerning how he was going to move forward with his treatments. Then, they both left.

As they began to walk to the car, Larry looked at Jennifer and noticed that all the blood looked like it had drained from her face. She was pale, and he asked her if she was okay.

"No! Larry, I'm not okay at this moment!" Jennifer said as she tried to hold back her tears. Larry grabbed her as they stood in the parking lot, both crying and holding each other as if that was their last moment together. Then, they got into the car, and Jennifer said, "Larry, I know in time that the Lord will see us both through this. We have to trust God. In His Word, He said He will never leave us nor forsake us, and He will be with us until the end. We totally have to continue to trust Him no matter what the outcome may be."

As they both sat there in the car for about ten minutes. Larry grabbed Jennifer's hand, and prayed. "Lord, Your will be done in me. I will not lose faith. I will not lose hope, for I know You will give us the strength to go through this. I will take up my cross and follow You, and I know that You will take care of my Jennifer."

Larry's Last Days

Larry decided to totally trust in God for his healing. Seeing that he was given a death sentence from the doctor, he wasn't going to take any chemo treatment at all. He discussed it with Jennifer, and she said, whatever he thought was best for him, she would accept and respect his decision. They decided to both pray together, and Jennifer would fast. Larry did not participate in the fasting. Due to the medications that he was taking, he needed to eat, although he lost weight no matter how much he ate.

Larry got weaker and weaker as the days went on. Jennifer would wait on him hand and foot even though the nurses would come in to do his cares, give him his medications, and provide sponge baths in the mornings.

He had a wonderful helper named Kathy that would come in and spend time with him when she was finished with his cares. She would flip the pages of the new *Better Homes and Gardens* magazines that Larry ordered. He had gotten so weak that he could not hold a book or flip the pages. She would read the articles from the magazine and lots of Bible scriptures to him as he laid there helpless but full of hope, knowing that God was good to him through the years. Kathy would call Jennifer in to help turn him every four hours so he wouldn't get bed sores on his body. Peggy would stop in and check on the both of them and sit with Jennifer because Larry was sleeping more. Sometimes, she would stop by just so Jennifer could get out to go grocery shopping or just to get a manicure. Jennifer decided she had to call all of his friends and his far away family members to come and see him before he passed away, and from time to time, one of his old friends would stop in to see him and say their goodbyes. By this time, Larry was skin and bones. He was getting close to crossing over to the other side of a new life. Jennifer had accepted the fact that Larry's life was over on this side of life, and she had cried so much that she did not think she had any more tears left. Her faith had grown so much by this time, and it was well with her and Larry.

God had given her the peace and the grace to do whatever she needed to do. She was sure that he would be with the Lord when he made that transition to other side. Jennifer always had a CD player next to him that played peaceful music, and she read the book of Psalms as he would go in and out of consciousness.

It was the weekend, and Larry had a different nurse on the weekends. Larry laid in the bed, awaking from a deep sleep. His eyes would open as he gasped for air with his oxygen going at full capacity. He felt like a fish out of water some days as death was slowly approaching, and he knew it. The hospice nurses came in to give him a sponge bath and take his temperature and blood pressure and give him his medication as needed.

"Hi, Larry. My name is Steve. I'm your weekend nurse. How are you doing today, sir?"

Each day was a battle for him. Larry said, "Well, I must take one day at a time. I really didn't think it would end like this for me, but it is well with my soul. God is still good all the time no matter what is going on health wise. I have had a good life, my own business, a beautiful loving wife. You see, I know what the end of my story is for me. Oh! Death, where is your sting?"

Then, Larry began to smile at Nurse Steve. "Yes, sir," Steve said. "I just pray when my time comes that I will have a good attitude like you have, sir. My faith isn't as strong as yours, but I'm working on it."

Larry said, "Well, I'll be praying for you that your faith will not fail you. You are young. You got some time."

Steve said, "Thank you, sir. I needed that. I'm supposed to encourage you, and you are encouraging me. Give me your arm, so I can take your blood pressure and temperature before we get started with your bath."

Larry looked at him and smiled and said, "We all need to be encouraged from time to time."

"Your temperature is normal, but your blood pressure today is low but we know why that is." Steve said, "Larry, I'm going to up your medication before I give you your bath, so you won't feel discomfort in any way."

Larry said, "Thank you!" Instantly, he felt better. He could not feel any pain anymore because he was on fifteen milligrams of morphine as needed and five more before his bath. As he was turning to his side to get his backside washed and lotion put on, Larry had nodded off to sleep and awakened in the room alone. The nurse had come and left for the day. Then, he thought to himself, *It won't be long now.* For he would see his mother and father that had passed away and were waiting for him with smiles on their faces. In his room, he was in and out of consciousness.

Larry would dream of himself as a little boy being baptized, running and playing with his friends and family at his church, remembering one of his favorite scriptures, the Lord saying I will be with you always. This was his Easter speech at the age of three. Larry would see himself lying in bed, but he wasn't sure if he was lying in bed because he was floating mid-air looking down at his own body. In his mind, he thought, *Wow! I'm having an out-of-body experience.* He didn't feel any pain at the time.

He was thinking to himself as he was in mid-air, *I like this! I feel great! No more pain.* As he looked down on himself in bed, he could see that he wasn't breathing anymore, and he thought to himself, *I'm dead!* But then, he thought about Jennifer, and he woke up in his own body. Larry laid there, thinking about what just happened. His bed was close to the window, so he could hear the birds singing as the warm sun would fill the room. He could hear the squirrels making that funny sound as they do when one is chasing the other. He knew he was still here on earth.

Jennifer walked into the room to check on him, asking him how he was feeling. He told her what had happened to him, and he asked her if it would be okay if he left now. Would she be okay? She took Larry's cool hands that were placed on his chest and held them and said, "Yes. I know the Lord will take care of me, and He will take care of you, too. You rest, my love. God will take care of me. Go in peace anytime you feel the Spirit. Don't quince it."

The following day, Jennifer woke up as usual and put a pot of coffee on before the nurse came in for the day to check on Larry to do his cares. His room was next to hers as she peeked in to see how he was doing. She could see that his skin was pale and he was still slowly breathing, but she knew it wouldn't be long. The morphine that he was taking kept him comfortable throughout the night. She jumped into the shower, and it hit her like a ton of bricks: the thought that it wouldn't be long before the Lord took her true love. Most days, she kept it together, but this wasn't one of them. She burst into tears uncontrollably, screaming as loudly as she could into the towels with her face in her hands. "Lord, I do thank You for this day, but I am feeling very fearful today, and I need Your peace. It's really hard to see that my husband is leaving me, but I have been missing him and will be missing him even more once he is gone. I will take comfort in knowing that You are with me always. Knowing that You would not put any more on me than I can bear."

Then, she began to wash her hair and face, pulling herself together and drying herself off and continuing to get dressed. She prayed that the Lord would give her strength she needed for today. She wasn't sure what the day would bring, but as always, the Lord would see her through.

Larry was having another out-of-body experience. He was at peace and praising God, saying in a whisper, "Thank you, Jesus," because he could barely breathe, but he was not in any pain. Larry now was having an out-of-body experience again. His body was still here, but his spirt seemed to be floating above. He was looking down upon himself lying on the bed once again, but it was hard for him to leave just yet. He wanted to say goodbye to Jennifer before he took his last breath. As his heartbeat began to fade, Jennifer was in the other room talking to her sister Peggy on the phone. She started to feel a presence in the room. She told Peggy that she would call her right back, but she needed to go and check on Larry.

She began to walk into the room to check on him, and Larry had opened his eyes and began to reach for her with his frail hands, taking deep breaths, speaking at a whisper, and letting her know that he loved her, and everything was going to be fine. As the tears began to fall down her face, he told her as he was looking into her eyes for the last time that he would be waiting for her on the other side of heaven. When her time came, he would be there to meet her, so don't be afraid and keep the faith. He smiled at her for the last time as a single tear fell out of his right eye.

Then, a blank stare came upon his face, and at that point Jennifer knew he was gone. The tears began to fall down her face when the doorbell rang. She knew it was the nurse coming to check on him, but he had departed from this life to the next one. She got up and left his side to open the door, then the nurse looked at her with the tears still falling down her face. She knew what had happened. She grabbed Jennifer and hugged her. Then, without one word, they went into Larry's room.

There he was, lying there with his eyes open and a slight smile on his face. His transformation was peaceful and painless. You could see it in his face. A tear of joy was left on his face as his spirit had left his body. There was no more pain for Larry. The nurse looked down at him with his eyes open. She gently put her hand over his face and closed his eyes, and then she told Jennifer he was in a better place and was at peace.

Jennifer said, "Yes, I know. I feel that he is. I need to make some phone calls."

"Yes, I know, but I would like to ask you some questions. But, before I ask you anything, I want to pray with you." Jennifer said that she would love that, so the nurse took her hand and prayed.

"Father God of love and mercy, embrace Jennifer, whose heart today overflows with grief and unanswered questions. Although she feels a sense of loss, comfort her as she expresses how she is feeling through her tears, fill her with Your peace and love always. This, I ask in Jesus' name. Amen."

She asked Jennifer if he had expired before she got up that morning. Jennifer told her no, that it just happened before the doorbell rang. The nurse looked down at her watch so she could get the time of death. She told Jennifer that it was routine, and that she would still have to check for a pulse and get him cleaned up so she could call the mortuary to pick up his body. Jennifer said that would be okay. She needed to call her sister Peggy.

Jennifer left the room, and before she could pick up the phone and dial her sister's number, the doorbell rang and it was Peggy. Jennifer told her she was just about to call her number because Larry had just passed away about thirty minutes ago. The nurse was in his room getting him ready to be picked up. Peggy grabbed her and gave her a hug. "Is there anything I can do for you, Jennifer?"

"Yes, can you go into the kitchen? I just put a fresh pot of coffee on. Could you get us a cup?"

She said okay, and then Peggy grabbed her again. The tears started falling down her face. She told her that she was sorry. She was going to miss her brother-in-law. He was a good man.

Jennifer said, "That's okay!" She knew where he was, and the Lord had given her enough time to prepare herself so it wouldn't be a shock for her. As the tears began to fall from her eyes, she told her sister that it was well, and she knew the Lord would never leave her nor forsake her, and she would grieve and really miss her husband.

This is not our permanent home on earth. It is a gift from God to enjoy each day here. It is just a gathering place for us to stop and decide if we want to go be with Christ. You see, He has given us all a choice to choose what we do with our time here on earth.

Larry left this life and crossed over into eternity where he will live forever with our Lord and savior, Jesus Christ.

My prayer is that each person that reads this book will face reality, knowing that each day that we live is a day closer to death. This life down here is not permanent and that one day we will have to face our Lord face-to-face, for every knee will bow and every tongue will confess that Jesus is Lord. My prayer is that we will be ready when our times come.

God so loved the world that He gave His only Son, and whosoever believes in Him should not perish but have everlasting life.

The End

Author Biography

Hi, my name is Patricia. I am a Christian author, and I love creative writing. My prayer is that, through my writings and by the grace of God, someone will be enlightened, encouraged, and healed from whatever life challenges they may be going through now or in the future. My stories are heartfelt, scripture-based, and inspirational. I write as the Spirit of the Lord leads me. Life can bring us the good, the bad, and the ugly, and it sometimes leaves us feeling lost and hopeless. I feel like there is an audience waiting for me and people that are assigned to me that need to hear my stories and the Word of God. There is no greater feeling than being made whole. I, too, have felt at times in my life lost, helpless, and hopeless, but God restored me. As a vessel of the Lord, I have a mandate to help comfort those who are lost, hurting, and those who have not given their lives to the Lord.

I am a mother and business owner, and through determination, I will retire and continue writing uplifting, encouraging, scripture-based, and inspirational stories, and even become a best seller. My books will help readers face some of life's toughest issues head on, bringing hope and peace, bringing words to life, giving them freedom through Jesus Christ. As I close my eyes, I see blank pages waiting to be filled. As words are being emptied into my ears and a is pen in my hand, I see myself writing.

Larry's Scriptures Book

1 Timothy 5:25 (KJV)

"Paul says, 'Drink no longer water, but use a little wine for thy stomach's sake and thine often infirmities.'"

Ephesians 6:12 (NIV)

"For our struggle is not against flesh and blood but against the rulers, against the authorities, against the powers of this dark world and against the spiritual forces of evil in the heavenly realms."

Matthew 18:20 (NIV)

"For where two or three gathers in my name, there am I with them."

Isaiah 41:10 (NIV)

"So do not fear, for I am with you; do not be dismayed, for I am your God. I will strengthen you and help you; I will uphold you with my righteous right hand."

Psalm 107:6 (NIV)

"Then they cried out to the Lord in their trouble,

And he delivered them from their distress."

Jeremiah 2:32 (NLT)

"Does a young woman forget her jewelry, or a bride her wedding dress? Yet for years on end my people have forgotten me."

CPSIA information can be obtained
at www.ICGtesting.com
Printed in the USA
BVHW040051270621
610451BV00006B/1606